Take up
Netball

Take up Sport

Titles in this series currently available or shortly to be published:

Take up Netball

Principal contributor:

Joyce Wheeler
Former England captain and coach;
manager of the England touring team

SPRINGFIELD BOOKS LIMITED

Copyright © Springfield Books Limited and White Line Press
1990

ISBN 0 947655 76 X

First published 1990 by
Springfield Books Limited
Springfield House, Norman Road, Denby Dale, Huddersfield
HD8 8TH

Edited, designed and produced by
White Line Press
60 Bradford Road, Stanningley, Leeds LS28 0EF

Editors: Noel Whittall and Philip Gardner
Design: Krystyna Hewitt
Diagrams: Chris Oxlade and Steve Beaumont

Printed and bound in Great Britain

Photographic credits
Cover photograph: Supersport
Supersport: 6, 9, 16, 17, 18, 24, 25, 29, 30, 32 (b), 33, 35,
43
Brian Worrell: 14
All other photographs by Iona LeCorre

Acknowledgements
Our thanks to the Surrey county players featured in the
instructional photographs.

Contents

1

Introduction

Origins of netball

Netball originated in America in 1891 as a form of basketball. In 1895 it was introduced into England by an American, Dr Toles, on a visit to the Physical Education College which is now at Dartford. In those days the goals were indeed baskets — the familiar rings with open-ended nets were not used until 1897. Quite appropriately the name "net ball" was used from about this time; the current form of "netball" as one word was not formally adopted until 1944.

In 1926 the All England Netball Association (AENA) was formed to administer the game in England; the International Federation of Women's Basketball and Netball Associations (IFWBNA), as the world governing body was originally called, was inaugurated in 1960. Since then netball has developed greatly, and is played widely throughout the United Kingdom, the Commonwealth countries, South Africa and Southeast Asia. There are many clubs which specialise in netball, and it is also one of the most popular games for girls and women in primary and secondary schools, colleges and universities. It is a very good way of keeping fit.

The majority of netball players are female, but there is no reason why it should not be played by men, and there are a few men's leagues in some areas. Also, mixed netball is sometimes played for fun, although in England such games are not recognised by the AENA.

Although the basic game originated in the USA, it is now almost unknown there, with just a few teams being found in areas where migrants from netball-playing countries have settled.

What is netball?

Netball is basically a running, chasing, passing and dodging game played by two teams of seven players. Goals are scored by throwing the ball through a horizontal ring defended by the other side.

Netball differs from many other team games in restricting the players to specific parts of the playing area, thus ensuring that the ball must be passed frequently.

Netball is played both indoors and outdoors, on hard-surfaced areas similar to tennis courts but a little larger (see Figure 1 on page 8).

The attraction of the game

Because the basic skills of catching and throwing are fairly easily mastered, new players soon begin to get satisfaction from the game. With slight modifications, such as reducing the court area or lowering the goals, a form of netball can be enjoyed by players of various ages, abilities and physiques.

With its great emphasis on teamwork, the game is a great way of teaching youngsters how to work together to achieve success. There is also plenty of scope for developing individual skills.

Netball is a fast and energetic game which satisfies many sporting needs: you can play as a sociable way of keeping fit, or be highly competitive at school, club, county or international level.

2

Requirements of the game

The netball court

The netball court should have a hard surface which is non-slip, porous, resilient and level. It should be clearly marked as shown in Figure 1.

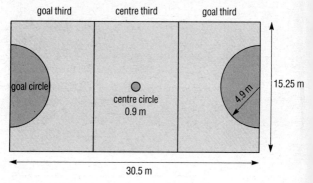

Figure 1 The court

The goals

Each goal consists of a post 3.05 m (10 ft) high with a tubular steel ring 380 mm (15 in) in diameter mounted 150 mm (6 in) below the top and projecting horizontally. A net, open at the end, hangs from the ring.

The ball

The ball is similar to a size five soccer ball. It may be made of leather, rubber or synthetic plastic, with a diameter of between 680 mm and 710 mm (27–28 in). The weight has to be between 397 g and 454 g (14–16 oz). Smaller and lighter balls may be used for young players.

The ball about to go through the ring during an England versus New Zealand match

Clothing

Netball clothing is simple and inexpensive. Most players wear a cotton sports shirt and skirt or shorts. These are all available in many attractive colours. Choose clothing which is an easy fit so that you can move freely and safely.

Footwear is important: netball puts a lot of pressure on your feet. You will be accelerating and changing direction many times during play, so your shoes need to fit really well. As you get into the game, you will decide what sort of boot or shoe will suit you best, but to start with, tennis shoes or trainers with good padding will be quite suitable. Whatever you use, the soles should be flat, with no spikes or studs.

If you are playing on an indoor wood surface, make sure that your shoes do not have black soles which will mark the floor.

Netball clothing is simple and inexpensive.

To avoid blisters, you need thick socks — the types with a looped pile are particularly comfortable. You can choose wool or cotton, but avoid nylon and other synthetics.

For outdoor games in a temperate climate, you will need a tracksuit to wear while you warm up before the game, and to avoid getting chilled afterwards. For indoor play, you will probably be able to manage with a sweater.

The only additional item of kit you will need is a bib which identifies your position of play (see page 11). These are usually provided by the organisers of your team.

Safety points
In order to prevent injury to yourself or your opponents, the following rules are strictly enforced:

● With the exception of a wedding ring, no jewellery at all may be worn when playing. If a wedding ring is worn, it must be covered by adhesive tape.

● The players' fingernails must be cut short.

Playing the game

Playing areas and positions

The court is divided into thirds, as shown in the diagram, and a semi-circle is marked in front of each goal. The players are restricted to certain areas. So that the players can be identified, they carry clear markings on their shirts, or wear marked bibs.

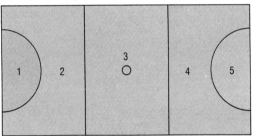

Figure 2 The playing areas of the court

The seven positions in each team are given in Table 1.

Table 1

Marking	Name	Permitted areas	Comment
GS	Goal Shooter	1 2	The only players allowed into the goal circle, and the only ones who may score
GA	Goal Attack	1 2 3	
WA	Wing Attack	2 3	
C	Centre	2 3 4	Centre-court players
WD	Wing Defence	3 4	
GD	Goal Defence	3 4 5	Defenders
GK	Goal Keeper	4 5	

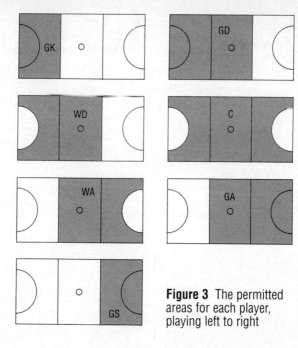

Figure 3 The permitted areas for each player, playing left to right

Figure 3 shows the areas in which the various players are allowed to operate. The teams are positioned so that it is natural for one attacking player in each side to be marked by a defender in the other. Only two players in a team, the Goal Shooter and Goal Attack, are permitted to enter the goal circle or to score.

Officials

Two umpires control the game; they stay outside the playing area, and each controls one half of the court. They do not change ends at any time. It is normal for the teams each to provide one of the umpires. Good

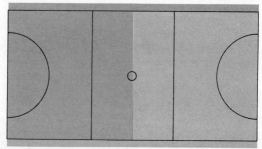

Figure 4 The two umpires control half the court and one sideline each.

umpires will try to keep the play flowing, and will not constantly blow the whistle for minor technical infringements which do not give either side an advantage.

Duration of a game

The game consists of one hour of play, divided into four quarters of 15 minutes each. After each quarter the teams change ends.

Intervals
A break, usually of three minutes, is taken between the first and second quarters, and between the third and fourth quarters. At half-time a ten-minute interval is allowed, but only if both teams agree to it! If it is very cold, windy or wet, the captains may want a much shorter break. If the teams request different lengths of half-time break, the umpires add the times together and divide by two: the result is the time allowed. So if team A want 8 minutes and team B wants 5 minutes, the umpires will re-start the game after 6½ minutes.

Tournament games
Sometimes one-day or weekend tournaments are held in which a large number of teams take part. In this case, shorter games are played, consisting of two halves, each of which lasts from five to twenty minutes.

Rules of the game

Playing the ball
There are strict rules about how you can play the ball:

● No kicking.

● No rolling the ball along the ground.

● You are not allowed to punch the ball with a clenched fist.

● No running with the ball.

● You must not attempt to play the ball from a sitting, kneeling or lying position.

● No handing the ball directly to a team-mate who is very close; your hands must be sufficiently far apart for an opponent to intercept without touching either of you.

● The ball may not be passed over a complete third of the court without being touched by at least one of the players.

Receiving the ball

When you are on the receiving end of a pass, there is another set of rules which affect you:

● You may "tip" the ball one or more times with your fingers or hand *before* getting it under control. Once you have control of the ball, you only have three seconds to pass it or shoot.

"Tipping" the ball like this is allowed, but once it is under control you have to pass it within three seconds.

● You are allowed to bounce the ball once (but not twice) before passing it to another player.

● You have to obey the footwork rules: basically, you have to stop as soon as you have caught the ball, and are then allowed only to move one foot, either in the direction of the pass or to pivot when throwing. See the panel for full details of just what you can do.

● If you fall when receiving the ball, you must stand up again before playing it. You have to do this all within three seconds.

Stopping suddenly when you receive the ball is one of the hardest skills for a netball player to master. You will be able to spot the expert players by the apparent ease with which they manage this and still keep in perfect balance.

Footwork rules

If you receive the ball with one foot grounded, or jump to catch and land on one foot, you can:

- step with the other foot in any direction, and then lift the landing foot, but you must pass or shoot before it is grounded again.

- pivot on your landing foot while you step with the other one as often as you like. If you then lift the pivoting foot, you must pass or shoot before re-grounding it.

- jump from your landing foot onto the other one, but you must throw the ball before you touch the ground again.

- step and jump with your non-landing foot, but again the ball must be thrown before you land.

If you receive the ball with both feet on the ground, or catch it when in the air and land on both feet simultaneously, you can:

- step with either foot in any direction. You can then lift the other foot, or jump, but you must throw the ball before the foot is grounded again.

- pivot on one foot while you step with the other any number of times. Once the pivoting foot is lifted, the ball must be thrown before it is grounded again.

- jump from both feet onto either foot, throwing the ball before the other foot is grounded.

The organisers of netball know that players will find a way of stretching the rules if they can, so the following moves are outlawed:

- Dragging or sliding the foot you land on
- Hopping
- Jumping from both feet and landing on both feet unless you have thrown the ball before you land

Remember, no matter how carefully you observe the footwork rules, you cannot retain possession of the ball for more than three seconds.

Receiving the ball with both feet off the ground

Starting play

At the start of play, the players must be in the positions shown in Figure 5: once the game is under way, they can move freely within their permitted areas.

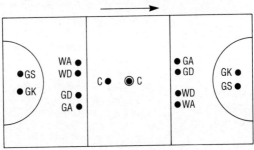

Figure 5 Positions at the start of play; the exact positions may vary to some extent.

The captains toss a coin to decide which team will start the game. The winner of the toss can choose either which goal to shoot at during the first quarter, or to make the first pass.

Opposing players move into action when the centre pass is made.

Play starts by one of the Centres making a pass from the centre circle. This first pass must be caught or touched by a player who is standing in the centre third, or who runs completely into it before taking the ball.

Scoring

A goal is scored by either the GS or GA throwing the ball through the ring from a position wholly within the goal circle. If any other player puts the ball through the ring, there is no score and play continues uninterrupted.

Out of play

The ball goes out of play when it touches the ground outside the court, or if the person holding or touching it is outside. Play is re-started by a throw-in which is taken where the ball crossed the line. The ball is thrown by an opponent of the team that last touched it, and she must be a player who is allowed to play in the third where the throw is taken.

A throw-in can be taken at the goal-line as well as at the sidelines. If thrown from the goal-line, the ball must go into the nearest third of the court. If thrown from the sideline, it must go into the nearest third or the one next to it. The thrower's feet must stay outside the line until the ball is released.

Interception and obstruction

Physical contact is not allowed in netball, and there are strict rules about what you can do to try to intercept the ball or to prevent an opponent from making an effective pass. You will not go far wrong if you don't attempt to intercept the ball or distract the player in possession of it unless you are at least 900 mm (3 ft) from her. The complete *Netball Rules* explain exactly how and when this distance is to be measured or judged, but you will soon get the feel of it in normal play.

The rules also stress the non-contact nature of the game, and it is up to you to avoid contact. Apart from avoiding obvious infringements, such as attempting to hold an opponent, you also have to keep clear of the path of a player who is moving too fast to stop. Needless to say, you are not allowed to grab the ball when it is in an opponent's possession.

In spite of the rules, two players will sometimes manage to get their hands on the ball at the same time! In this case, the matter is settled by a toss-up between the two players involved.

Penalties

If you break any of the rules, one of the following penalties will be awarded against you:

Penalty pass or penalty shot

A penalty pass is awarded for contact or obstruction. The penalty takes the form of a pass from where the offender was standing. Any member of the opposing team who is allowed in that third of the court may make the pass, and the offender must stand clear to one side of the thrower until the ball is clear of her hands.

If the offence occurred in the goal circle to the GA or GS, either a pass or a direct shot at goal may be taken.

Free pass

A free pass is the penalty for individual offences such as offside and playing the ball incorrectly. It is taken in the same way as a penalty pass, but the opposition may defend in the normal manner, and no direct shot at goal is allowed.

When taking a penalty or free pass, the ball may not be thrown over a complete third of the court without being touched by another player.

Toss-up

A toss-up puts the ball back into play after a simultaneous offence occurs — for example, two players going offside together, or if the umpire cannot decide who last touched the ball before it went out of play.

For the toss-up, two opposing players stand facing each other, looking towards their own goal ends. They should be 900 mm (3 ft) apart, with their arms at their sides. An umpire holds the ball between them at about shoulder height, blows a whistle and simultaneously flicks the ball a short distance into the air. The players can try to catch it, or they can hit it clear with a hand. They must not move until the whistle is blown.

Offside

You are offside if you move into a playing area which is not designated for your position, regardless of whether you have the ball. You are permitted to reach over and take the ball from an offside area — even leaning on the ball if necessary — provided that you don't touch the ground there.

Simultaneous offside

If you go offside at the same time as an opponent, and neither of you has the ball, you both move back into your permitted area at once, and play continues. However, if either or both of you has the ball, or even just touches it, a toss-up is taken in your own area between you and the opponent.

In the exceptional case where a player who is allowed only in the goal third goes offside into the centre third at the same moment that an opponent goes offside into the goal third, one or both players being in contact with the ball, a toss-up is taken in the centre third between any two opposing players allowed in that area!

The toss-up

Advantage

An umpire will not stop the game or award a penalty for a minor offence if to do so would put the non-offending team at a disadvantage. Similarly, the position from which a penalty pass is taken may be altered slightly in the interests of fairness.

The rules given in this section will enable you to play a fair game of netball, but they are by no means complete. A full set of the official rules, which will settle all arguments, is available from the All England Netball Association (see page 48) or from your national governing body.

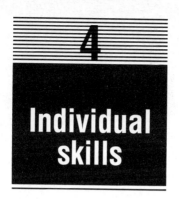

Individual skills

Effective netball calls for a blend of skills:

- Ball control
- Footwork and balance
- Catching
- Throwing

Ball control

The first step in getting enjoyment from playing netball is learning to handle and control the ball.

If you start by holding and tossing the ball, you will soon become familiar with its weight, size and texture. Then try bouncing the ball, varying the height and force of the bounce. This gets you used to the part your fingers, wrists and arms play in controlling the ball.

One-hand exercise

This simple exercise is great for developing both ball control and balance. Simply hold the ball on one hand with your fingers spread around it, and move it around your body, varying the height from above your head right down to floor level. Constantly vary the distance of the ball from your body, sometimes taking it as far away as you can reach. Don't drop the ball! You will soon be using a relaxed and flexible movement as you control the twisting of your wrist and arm.

Keep practising the one-hand exercise until you can do it fast and confidently with either hand.

Two-hand exercise

For netball you will need to develop a firm but flexible two-handed grip on the ball. Practise this by holding the ball between your hands and swinging it to either side of your body, high and low. Do this with your arms both bent and straight. Speed up until you can snap the ball fast into different positions without dropping it. You can introduce variety by jogging or running while handling the ball.

Footwork and balance

Netball is played in a very small area, and so — as well as being able to run fast — you must be able to change speed and direction rapidly if you are to make the most of it. The key to this is good footwork, which will enable you to move around the court economically while maintaining the control and balance that you need.

Because you are not allowed to run with the ball in netball, you must be able to stop suddenly without losing your balance. The way to do this is to bring the weight of your body down over a stable base — that means right over one or both of your feet.

Footwork practices

You can use a variety of short-distance running exercises. Here are a couple to start with, but try to invent some of your own, too:

● *Change-stride sprints*. Run the length of the court using steps of many different sizes; change your stride length every three steps. Make your long strides really long, and the short ones very short.

● *Dodging sprints*. Run in different directions: forwards, backwards, sideways and diagonally.

You can perform all these practices on your own, but it is more fun to work with others if you can. You will soon find ways of making the exercises competitive!

Jumping and landing practices

● *Touch-the-net*. Run from the goal-circle line, and jump to try to touch the net at a goal. After a few tries, make it a rule not to move your feet immediately after you have landed. Be sure to bend your knees on landing so that you don't jar your back.

● *Pair jumps*. Jump as high as you can with a partner. You each stretch upwards with your hands when you jump, and aim to touch the tips of your partner's fingers.

● *Jump from either foot*. Whenever you are practising jumps, vary the foot you use, so that you will be able to react rapidly during play.

Using your footwork

You will have to match your footwork to the demands of the game. Use it to make the best of the space you have, keeping in mind the following points:

● the restricted area in which you are allowed to play (see Figure 3).

You can practise pair jumps with the ball or without it.

Catching the ball and making a one-footed landing

- the position of your opponents. For example, if someone is limiting your movement, try to make space for yourself by using your feet to draw her in one direction and then dodging quickly round her.

- the position of the receiver. When you have the ball and are going to pass, you can decide whether to run right or left, according to the space into which the receiver is moving.

Catching

Catching is an important part of netball — you won't enjoy much of the play if your team-mates can't trust you to receive a pass safely.

These points will help you to become a safe catcher:

- Watch the ball to judge its flight and speed.

- Prepare your body and hands to receive the ball — get behind or underneath the flight of the ball, and reach out towards it.

- Curve and spread your fingers so that they will cup the ball safely.

- As soon as you contact the ball, bring it towards your body.

You can practise catching on your own by bouncing the ball against a wall, but it is much easier in a small group. With a few friends you can pass the ball to one another; you will soon develop the skill of catching the ball safely and firmly at various heights. You also need to be in a group to practise catching when running and jumping — important skills of the game.

Practise catching with either hand and with both hands together. Learn to take the ball at full stretch to either side of your body as well as high above your head. Get used to gathering up low bounces, too; this is a skill which is often overlooked by beginners, yet it is often an easy way of getting possession during a match.

A stylish high two-handed catch

Throwing

Once you have possession of the ball, you need to be able to throw it accurately. Just as with catching, you can practise by bouncing the ball against a wall, but the best way is with a partner or in a group.

You will almost certainly have learned to throw a ball long before you became interested in netball, but to be able to pass it smoothly every time when under pressure from other players needs a lot of practice. You must first get used to taking up a good starting position without having to think about it (see panel).

Starting position

- Get well-balanced, with your weight evenly distributed over your feet.

- Hold the ball close to your body, using both hands.

Ready for the chest pass — a good starting position

Shoulder throw

The most common throw in netball is from just above shoulder-level, and like many of the other throws, can be made either one-handed or two-handed. From the starting position:

- Turn your body sideways, transferring your weight onto your back foot.

- Raise the ball up and slightly back, above your rear shoulder.
- Transfer your weight onto your front foot, which should be pointing in the direction of the throw. Your back foot should stay on the ground.
- Follow through: your throwing arm, shoulder and fingers should all be in line with the catcher as the ball is released.
- Keep the whole action smooth and continuous.

The shoulder throw

High shoulder throw
This is very similar to the shoulder throw, but the ball starts from above your head. It is essential against a tall player who is making an energetic defence.

Underarm throw
This is a low throw in which the ball is taken back below your waist and released at that level. A fast underarm pass is deceptive and hard to intercept.

Bounce pass
A bounce pass is a good way of getting the ball past a player who defends well in the air. The action is shorter and sharper than for the direct throws. Aim the ball downwards, and put some energy into it. Ideally it will bounce just behind or beside the feet of your opponent before being gathered safely by the catcher.

Chest pass
This is a two-handed throw from chest height. It should be fast and accurate, but you need to be almost facing the catcher.

- Hold the ball in front of your chest, with your wrists bent back and your fingers and thumbs spread widely behind it. Your elbows will need to be quite high and out to the sides of your body.

- Throw the ball by extending your arms, wrists and fingers strongly forward in the direction of the throw.

- Give a final flick with the fingers as the ball goes on its way.

The chest pass

Throwing — where, when and how?

Where to throw

- In the direction the receiver is moving.

- *Ahead* of the receiver, so that the ball may be caught with extended arms and out of the reach of the opponents.

When to throw

- When you are on-balance.

- When you have sized up the situation for just long enough to make sure that you are not going to pass the ball straight into the hands of an opponent.

- When the receiver's final move to dodge her opponent appears to have been made.

How to throw

This will depend on all sorts of things, and as your skill develops you will have a wider choice. At first you should keep to simple throws which you can perform accurately — if you are a natural right-hander, there's no point in attempting left-handed throws if you don't really know where they will end up! However, do keep practising until you can throw well with either hand.

While you are still quite new to the game, remember that a safe short pass is usually a better choice than a chancy long one.

Shooting

The finest teamwork in the world will be wasted if the GA or GS cannot put the ball through the ring! Even if you do not think that you are very likely to play in either of the scoring positions, you should try to master the basic skills of shooting, just in case.

The basic skills needed are good balance and sound judgement of distance.

The basic standing shot

● Adopt the correct starting position: your weight should be distributed evenly over both feet, which can be side by side or one in front of the other.

● Hold the ball with your palm upturned and your fingers spread towards you. The ball should rest on the base of your fingers and thumb — not on the palm.

● You can use one hand or two.

● Keep your weight over your feet until you have released the ball.

● Now shoot, concentrating on the ring the whole time.

● Hold the ball high above your head, with your knees and elbows slightly bent.

● Push upwards from your feet, extending your arms.

● Release the ball as high as possible.

● Project the ball upwards to the ring with your wrists and fingers; as it leaves your hands your fingers give it a final flick.

The standing shot

Of course, you don't always have the chance to stand still for a shot at goal, but with slight adjustments to the timing, strength of release and direction, the basic shooting action can be used in running, step-back and round shots.

When you are practising shots at goal, start close to the post and then gradually move further away as your accuracy improves. If the goal feels altogether too high at first, simply practise throwing the ball over a high rope or obstacle. If you have a partner, you can turn this into a shooting and catching practice.

Attacking

When you are attacking, your aim is to pass the ball quickly and safely towards the goal. To be successful at this you need a variety of skills to get you clear of your opponents. You will find that you have to make some very rapid decisions.

When you have the ball, try to:

● be aware of space which is free and in which you can move.

● re-position into an appropriate space once your throw has been made.

● keep your opponents guessing — don't signal your movement in advance.

● be decisive — avoid jumping up and down on the spot or rocking from side to side.

● use your body to fake your intention: *the feint dodge.*

England Captain Jillian Hipsey looks for space to pass.

When you are about to receive the ball, prepare by:

- standing in a balanced position with your weight over the balls of your feet.
- keeping your knees slightly bent, so that you are ready to move.
- waiting until the thrower is ready to throw before making a final sprint to receive the ball.

Be ready to make any of these moves:

- a sudden sprint into a selected unmarked space.
- a sudden sprint with a sudden stop.
- a sudden sprint, change direction and sprint again.
- a sudden sprint, slow down and then sprint again.
- a feint dodge. Take a deliberate step which draws your opponent in one direction, and then sprint another way.

A Centre takes the ball on the move with a successful dodge.

Defending

At some stage in the game, every player has to defend. The aim of the defender is to get possession of the ball by forcing the attacker to make mistakes, and to keep the attacker out of the game by pressurising her and limiting the amount of space in which she can move.

Fast reactions are essential for effective defence: you can best develop these by practice. Learn to watch the path of the ball and the moves of the players as the ball is passed towards the goal. Practise turning very quickly in different directions, sometimes using the pivot turn.

Defence can change to attack very fast, and the key to this is gaining possession of the ball. If you can intercept and stop an attacker from getting the ball, you can start an attacking move yourself. To do this, you must always be ready to react quickly to the situation and to take any opportunity to catch, deflect or intercept a pass.

You can practise reaction and interception with the help of a wall. Stand with your back to the wall and throw the ball behind you against the wall; turn fast and catch the ball as it rebounds. Vary the way you throw the ball — sometimes to the right or left of your body, and sometimes above your head.

More fun can be had by working with partners. Take turns to be the defender, and try to snatch the ball when it is dropped or bounced into the space around you.

To defend effectively, you have to be familiar with the techniques of defending:

The covering position

This is a basic position which you should get thoroughly used to. Look for the following points:

● You should be positioned between your opponent and the ball.

● Your shoulder should be covering one of your opponent's shoulders.

● You should stay close to your opponent, but not touching her.

● Keep your head turned sideways, so that you can see both your opponent and the ball at all times.

● Be poised on the balls of your feet, ready to move with small, quick steps to maintain the covering position.

From this basic covering position, you are able to frustrate your opponent's efforts to get free or to pass the ball. You can also intercept or deflect a pass being made by springing and extending your body and arms into the path of the ball.

Keep the right distance

While you are covering a player who is not in possession of the ball, you can be as close as you wish without actually touching her. Once she receives the ball, you must stay at least 900 mm (3 ft) away. Use quick, small steps to shadow the player and adjust the distance.

The covering position

Below: *Tight marking and covering close to the goal*

Interception

Naturally, the object of covering a player is to prevent her from passing effectively if she receives the ball, and to get the ball yourself if you can. Good positioning and speed are needed:

- Face the thrower, feet slightly astride and knees slightly bent.

- Hold your arms ready to intercept, deflect or block the ball.

- Anticipate if you can: just before your opponent releases the ball, attempt to intercept by jumping and thrusting out your arms.

This action is also used when defending against a shot at goal. You should be able to anticipate that the ball is going towards the goal post, which makes positioning slightly easier, but watch out for fake passes and feints made by the shooter. After a shot which you have failed to intercept, turn quickly so that you have a good chance of catching the ball if it rebounds from the goal post.

Once you have mastered the basic defending skills, you will be able to adapt them so that you can intercept balls being passed on either side of your body, and balls at different heights.

Spirited interception to save a goal

Mark the space
It is often effective to mark a particular player and to try to shadow all her movements. However, it is sometimes better to mark the *space* she will need to move into, rather than the actual player — this can lure her into a false sense of security, as she thinks she is free! Keep between her and the usable space as much as you can. If you manage this really well, your opponent can find it very difficult to play an effective part in the game.

Winning the toss-up

When the umpire flicks the ball into the air in a toss-up, you need a very quick snatching action to catch it before your opponent.

Take up a comfortable position facing your opponent, with your arms by your sides. You should have your weight over the balls of your feet, which may be side by side or one in front of the other.

Watch the ball — not the umpire! Respond as soon as the whistle blows and the ball is released. If you can gather the ball safely, pull it towards your body at once. Alternatively, bat the ball to one side, but make sure that a player from your team is there to catch it.

Set up practice situations with a few friends and find out who is fastest at getting the ball in a toss-up.

Good teamwork on both sides as the Trinidad WD makes a high catch against Australia

5

Working as a team

So far we have concentrated on developing the individual skills you need to be able to play netball; now we learn how the seven players together can use these skills to operate as an effective team. This requires you to work together smoothly — both in attack to secure goals, and in defence to counter the opposition's moves. This does not mean that the team has to work like a machine: the players should still be able to retain their individuality and make their own decisions.

Principles of teamwork

Overall

- Make the abilities of the individual contribute to a cohesive unit.

- Ensure that every move has a purpose.

- Watch the ball all the time.

- Vary your play so that it does not become predictable.

- Interchange with each other where necessary.

- Study the opposition's play.

In attack

- Use the space your team-mates leave to receive the ball.

- Be prepared to move out of an area to leave it free for a team-mate who will be able to use it more effectively than yourself.

In defence

- Work together to harass the opposition so that they have to use less familiar skills to deal with the situation.

Positions and responsibilities

In netball the positions of the players are very closely defined, and so are their responsibilities. You will have a specific role to play according to your area and playing position. Here are the responsibilities of each player:

GK Goal Keeper

- To mark the opposing GS closely, both inside and outside the goal circle.
- To leap to intercept or deflect all kinds of passes.
- To intercept shots at goal with a well-timed jump.
- To gather missed shots as they rebound.
- To link with your GD and/or WD in the goal third to initiate an attacking move.

GD Goal Defence

- To be able to use all forms of defence skill.
- To prevent the opposing GA from receiving the ball in a position from which she could score.
- To anticipate the path of the ball and try to intercept it.
- To join in your own team's attack.

WD Wing Defence

- To prevent the opposing WA from progressing towards the goal, and to limit her ability to pass the ball into the goal circle.
- To be able to move quickly in all directions, particularly backwards.
- To receive the centre pass and pass the ball on accurately.

C Centre

- To initiate the moves at the start of play.
- To be a link player between attack and defence.
- Both to attack and to defend by using sudden quick changes of direction.
- To know when to move out and leave the space free.
- To back up play around the goal circles.

WA Wing Attack

- To make accurate passes into the goal circle.

- To develop a good sense of timing and position, and so to move into the best place for accurate passes.
- To use a variety of dodges in general play.
- To make the best of the centre pass.
- To receive the ball, facing the attacking goal circle.

GA Goal Attack

- To work with the C and WA to bring the ball to the goal circle.
- To time the move into the goal circle.
- To use a variety of shooting techniques.
- To co-operate with the GS to use the goal circle effectively.
- To catch rebounds after missed shots.

GS Goal Shooter

- To shoot with consistent accuracy as well as variety.
- To be able to dodge in a confined space and move at the right time to achieve a good scoring position.
- To be able to catch the ball at different heights with either hand or both together.
- Like the GA, to be good at catching rebounds after missed shots.

Hints for beginners

Before you make your mind up, try playing in all the positions so that you can decide which you prefer. If you are happy in a particular position, you will probably do best in it.

Get used to defending against your opposite player.

Working together

You must learn to work together with the six other players, using the basic skills of movement, catching and throwing to pass the ball successfully to the goal. Remember, when you have the ball, you always have the choice of two players who are able to receive it.

Figure 6 illustrates some simple systems of organising the team to cover the court space efficiently and economically. You need to hold plenty of practice sessions to develop routines to determine who will receive the ball in certain conditions. This all helps to build up team cohesion and confidence.

However, as the situation is constantly changing according to the play of the opposition and the position of your own team-mates, you cannot be too rigid in your plans. Good team play allows lots of flexibility in both moves and passes.

On some moves down the court, not all the members of the team will touch the ball, but they will still have a positive part to play by creating space in which their team-mates can move and receive the ball.

For any move to be successful and to result in a goal, the players need to know how to get free from their markers at the *right time* and in the *right space*.

A simple way of starting to build effective team play is by dividing the team into smaller units which then practise working together within the limits of their playing areas. Each unit is initially responsible for passing and playing the ball in a third of the court.

Here are examples of some of these units:

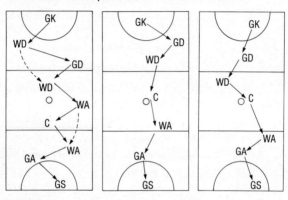

Figure 6 Team-play routines for passing the ball down the court

To make the most of this practice system, the units should move the ball from one third to another as efficiently as possible. The practice should include different starting points, for example:

● from a throw-in at the sideline

● from a throw-in from the backline

● from a free pass or penalty pass

● from a toss-up

Figure 7 shows some example passing routines.

From these basic patterns of play, simple inter-changes may be made. This means that, for a short time, two players will adopt the responsibilities and roles of each other. Usually the interchange is made between two players who are able to play in at least two areas of the court. Figure 8 gives one example of such an inter-change.

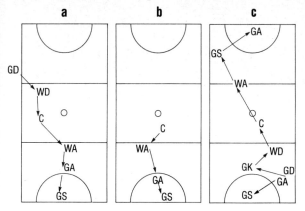

Figure 7 Passing routines from (a) a throw-in, (b) a free pass, (c) a toss-up

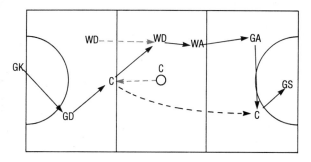

Figure 8 The C has exchanged with the WD, who moves into the centre third to link with the WA. After passing the ball, the C will run to the end of the court to link with the GA and GS.

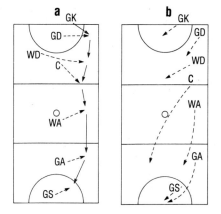

Figure 9 Players' movements (a) to receive a pass, and (b) after the pass has been made

In all these practices, you must get used to the idea that team play means much more than simply passing the ball to the right player. Once you have passed, you should always assist play by covering the court space and being ready to support your team-mates, or to intercept rapidly if the opposition attempts a sudden break — see Figure 9 (page 39).

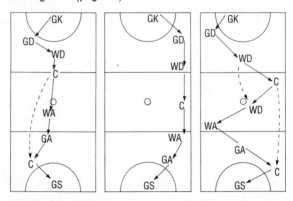

Figure 10 Varied practice routines for getting the ball down the court

Keep variety in the practices by moving alternately to right or left, and changing the height and angle of the first pass. You will soon be passing the ball the length of the court using different combinations of players.

Centre passes

If your team is to make the centre pass, it automatically becomes the *attacking* team. You must keep this advantage by confidently maintaining possession after the initial move. The starting positions of the teams are extremely important if this aim is to be achieved. Your team must have players ready and able to move into the centre third. Remember, as attackers your team-mates should always have the advantage of knowing where, when and how they are going to move.

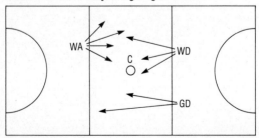

Figure 11 Available pathways for WA to receive the centre pass; pathways for GD and WD are also shown

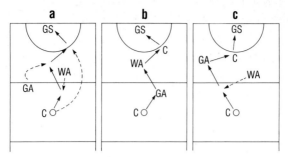

Figure 12 Some possible sequences of play from the centre pass: (a) a simple order of play; (b) the ball takes the same path, but the player order is different; (c) this time the ball's path is different, while the player order has reverted to that in (a).

When the team starts working well together, you will find that you are automatically adapting all these routines to different situations in the game — throw-ins, penalty passes and free passes.

Note for coaches: teamwork for beginners
Beginners haven't the experience to make many rapid decisions, so concentrate on these points:

● Keep the tactics simple.

● Require the player to make one clear move at a time: for example, to get the ball or to move into a space.

● Help the players to time their moves accurately.

● Remind the players to move into a space as soon as they've passed the ball.

● At the throw-in, have the ball passed into the court rather than along the sideline.

6

Special games for youngsters

If it will mean that young players will be able to partici-
pate in the game more fully, and so get more enjoyment from it, you can easily adapt the rules:

● The adult game may be adapted by playing in one-
third or two-thirds of the court — it is only necessary to move a goalpost.

● Each team may be reduced to three, four or five
players.

● The permitted areas of play can be altered, so that
greater freedom is allowed. This gives the new-
comers plenty of opportunities to throw and catch
before having to worry too much about just *where*
they can play.

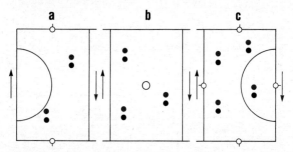

Figure 13 Three adapted games using one-third of the
court each.

In (a), 2 v 2, the players simply aim to get the ball into
the goal — anyone may score.

In (b), 3 v 3, there are no goals: the ball must be caught
over the sidelines to score, and every member of the
team must have received it before it gets to the sideline.

In (c), 4 v 4, each team can aim for the nearest goal only
after a set number of passes — three, for example.

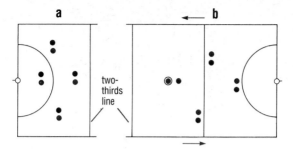

Figure 14 In these adapted 4 v 4 games, the court is divided into two unequal parts.

In (a) — one-third of the court — both teams are aiming to score in the one goal. The ball starts from the two-thirds line, and four passes must be made by either team before shooting is allowed from within the circle. After a goal, the non-scoring team starts again from the two-thirds line.

In (b), the remaining two-thirds of the court, play is started from the centre circle, and the attacking team has to try to score a goal. If the defending team intercepts, they have to get the ball to the two-thirds line in order to score a point. After each goal or point, the teams swap over roles, and the game starts from the centre again.

These junior-school players are enjoying a lively game on a reduced-size court.

7

Fitness

You will be surprised at how much physical effort is needed to play netball well. A team in which all the members are fit enough to maintain maximum effort until the end of the final quarter will almost always beat opponents who are less fit.

Fitness training should be an important part of your team preparation. It need not be boring, and if the exercises are chosen carefully they will also improve your netball skills.

You will get the best results if you organise your fitness training so that you practise individual skills for specific lengths of time, rather than doing what you happen to feel like. A simple example would be to divide a half-hour team session into 15 minutes of throwing and catching followed by 15 minutes of chasing games.

Warm-up and warm-down

Before both training sessions and matches, you must get your body ready for the effort by warming up its joints and muscles.

Warm-up
A few minutes spent stretching carefully and jogging are all that is needed. Pay particular attention to the joints and areas of the body upon which netball makes special demands — ankles, legs, hips, back and arms.

During the practice session or match
Take the opportunity to perform simple stretching movements which include all the main muscle groups during intervals or lulls in play. This helps to relax the muscles, which increases their efficiency and avoids stiffness and pain.

Warm-down
Don't let your body cool off too quickly after practice sessions or a game. Put on a sweater or tracksuit, and

jog gently for a minute or two before going into the dressing-room. If you have the opportunity, do take a shower after any sort of energetic exercise.

Figure 15 Some simple flexibility exercises

calf

thigh and hips

hamstrings

shoulders

back

lower back

hips and buttocks

hamstrings

Circuit training

A circuit consists of a number of different exercises which are performed one after the other and then repeated. This can be an excellent way of preparing your body for netball. As well as general exercises for developing stamina, such as repeated step-ups and star jumps, you should include plenty of activities which will develop your agility and improve your throwing skills. Skipping, hopping, repeated short sprints across the court, and multiple throws and catches against a wall, are all good exercises to include in a circuit for netball.

Circuits need to be developed carefully to suit the age and capabilities of the players.

8

How the game is run

In England, netball is administered by the All England Netball Association (AENA) and the English Schools Netball Association (ESNA), which are closely linked. In most other netball-playing countries there are similar links between school and national organisations. The other national governing bodies in the UK are the Scottish Netball Association (SNA), the Northern Ireland Netball Association (NINA), and the Welsh Netball Association (WNA).

Netball is a popular game. In England alone, there are more than three thousand clubs, spread throughout ten regions which are sub-divided into counties. AENA competition leagues are organised at club, county, regional and national levels; the other national associations omit the county or regional levels.

Coaching and umpiring

Most UK national associations and regions run coaching and umpiring courses, and the WNA holds a regular conference on coaching and umpiring. For young players (16–21), there are six centres of excellence established throughout England, where the players receive expert coaching in all aspects of the game.

The AENA has a range of awards for coaching, umpiring and shooting. It also publishes *Netball*, a quarterly magazine which gives details of the latest training schemes as well as competition news and results.

Other national governing bodies throughout the world provide similar courses and awards, and many produce their own publications.

Joining a club

The clubs play in different leagues, according to how competitive they are: some are purely recreational; some concentrate on playing as a way of keeping fit; some are strictly competitive. Many clubs are formed by old girls from certain schools, while businesses and shops often have clubs of their own. New members, regardless of age and ability, are welcomed by all clubs, and many have special sections for youngsters of ten and upwards.

As there are so many clubs, you should not have much difficulty finding one which will suit you. In England, the AENA will provide addresses and information concerning the regional and county associations, which in turn will give you information about clubs in your area. Alternatively, try contacting your local Sports Council office, or ask at the nearest sports centre or public library. Readers in other countries should contact their own national governing body.

Very few clubs have their own premises — normally they play at local schools, parks or sports centres. There are usually training sessions and matches at least once a week, at times to suit the members; daytime sessions to which mothers can take young children are increasingly well supported. Club membership is generally very inexpensive and no highly specialised clothing is needed.

While you may be quite happy to play locally, if you are more ambitious you can aim for county, regional or national honours. Championships at these levels are organised annually for both school and adult teams. The ultimate aim for the keenest player is to be in the team which wins the four-yearly World Tournament.

Useful addresses

British Isles

All England Netball Association
Francis House
Francis Street
London
SW1P 1DE

English Schools Netball
    Association
c/o Ms J Bracey
76 Macklands Way
Rainham
Kent
ME3 4PF

The Northern Ireland Netball
    Association
9 Thomas Street
Belfast
BT15 1FF

The Republic of Ireland Netball
    Association
Genazzano
Bird Avenue
Clonskeagh
Dublin 14

The Scottish Netball Association
Kelvin Hall Sports Centre
Argyle Street
Glasgow
G3 8AA

The Welsh Netball Association
3rd Floor
3 Westgate Street
Cardiff
South Glamorgan
CF1 1JF

Overseas

The Australian Netball Association
99 Awaba Street
Mosman
NSW 2088

The Canadian Amateur Netball
    Association
36 Windermere Crescent
St Albert
Alberta
T8N 355

The New Zealand Netball
    Association
41 Kowhai Avenue
Upper Hutt

The United States Netball
    Association
680 East 92nd Street
Brooklyn
New York
NY 11236

International

The International Federation of Netball Associations
99 Awaba Street
Mosman
NSW 2088
Australia